Who cares?

The parable of the good Samaritan

Diane Walker

Acknowledgments

We would like to thank Wylva Davies and Val Bulman for their help. We would also like to express our gratitude to the following schools for trialling the material.

St Mark's C of E, Worsley, Manchester
Parkview Primary, Oakwood, Derby
St Andrew's Primary, Salisbury
Holy Trinity Primary, Bradley Stoke, Bristol

THE
STAPLEFORD
CENTRE

The Stapleford Centre is an interdenominational centre which aims to produce materials, and offer in-service courses, to resource the teaching of Christianity in schools. Full details of courses and publications are available from:

The Stapleford Centre
The Old Lace Mill
Frederick Road
Stapleford
Nottingham
NG9 8FN
Tel: 0115 939 6270
Fax: 0115 939 2076
E-mail: admin@stapleford-centre.org
Website: www.stapleford-centre.org

Text copyright © Diane Walker 2001
Illustrations copyright © Jane Taylor 2001

The author asserts the moral right
to be identified as the author of this work

Published by
The Bible Reading Fellowship
First Floor, Elsfield Hall
15–17 Elsfield Way, Oxford OX2 8FG
ISBN 1 84101 204 1
First published 2001
10 9 8 7 6 5 4 3 2 1 0
All rights reserved

Acknowledgments
Unless otherwise stated, scripture quotations are taken from the Good News Bible published by
The Bible Societies/HarperCollins Publishers Ltd, UK © American Bible Society 1966, 1971, 1976,
1992, used with permission.

A catalogue record for this book is available from the British Library

Printed and bound in Malta

Contents

How to use this book

This book provides the following:
* ★ Masters for a Big Book
* ★ Activities for literacy work (word, sentence and text level)
* ★ RE follow-up ideas
* ★ RE activity sheets/stimulus material
* ★ Differentiated RE activities
* ★ Ideas for reflection/learning from religion

Parables

Parables are stories with a spiritual/moral meaning. They are an example of non-literal language, along with metaphors and similes.

RE and literacy work

As well as the Big Book masters, this book contains a bank of activities at word, sentence and text level; literacy activity sheets; RE follow-up and RE activity sheets. There is some information for teachers on some of the activity sheets; this can be removed using office 'white-out' before copying. The material in this book can be used in RE and literacy time but the focus will be different in literacy and RE. Literacy teaching should not replace RE; neither should RE replace literacy teaching.

The Big Book

The story can be used in RE or literacy time. The masters for the Big Book can be used in a number of ways:
* ★ Photocopied on to acetates
* ★ Enlarged and photocopied to create a Big Book
* ★ Photocopied to create small pupil books

The pictures can be coloured either by hand or by scanning into the computer and using a paint programme on parts of the drawings. (Some software can do this.)

Suggested activities

* ★ Use items in the text to tell the story.
* ★ Pupils can mime or role-play situations in the story.
* ★ Ask questions about possible consequences of actions and what might happen next.
* ★ Bring out any moral issues for discussion: 'Do you think the Levite was right to…?'
* ★ Ask pupils to read sections with appropriate expression.
* ★ Ask their opinion about what is happening in the story.
* ★ Relate the issues in the stories to pupils' experiences.

QCA links (England)

Parables link to the following units in the QCA RE schemes: 1D, 2B, 3C, 3D, 5C, 5D, 6C and 6F.

Handling biblical material

Pupils should be told where the story comes from and why it is important to Christians. Christian material should be introduced: 'Today we are looking at a story from the Bible (or based on a story from the Bible) which is important to Christians.' This allows pupils to identify with the story or to study it from another perspective.

Who cares?

Once there was a man called Jude who had to travel from Jerusalem to Jericho on the road that leads through the hills.

Some smooth and level roads run through green farmland. Walkers can stroll along and take their time, chatting to the workers in the fields. Some roads run through towns and villages, and travellers can always find someone to share a meal with them, or to give them cool water on a hot day.

But the road from Jerusalem to Jericho was a
wild and dangerous track. It snaked along
the rocky hillsides, climbing so
steeply that travellers had no
breath left for chatting. No
one lived there who would
offer them a drink or
a meal.

However, some people did live there. Invisible among the
rocks and caves lived robbers. All day they would hide among
the rocks, waiting for travellers to come struggling up the
track. Then they would attack. Sometimes, they left their
victim with his life. Often, they took even that.

Because of the danger, people who had to go from Jerusalem to Jericho always tried to travel in groups. Few people were brave – or foolish – enough to walk that way alone. But Jude had to travel, and he had to travel that day. He could not find anyone to go with him, and he could not wait.

So he set off alone. 'I shall be all right!' he thought. 'I'll hurry. By the time the robbers know I am there, I will be safe on the other side of the hills.'

He set off walking briskly. It was a hot day, and the road was steep. He began to walk more and more slowly. The road narrowed, and became nothing more than a rough track. 'Surely I will reach the top of the hill soon,' he said to himself. But the track still climbed ahead of him, and he could not see the end of it. 'I shall have to stop for a rest!' he thought, and sat down on a rock, panting for breath.

High above him an eagle circled, scanning the rocks below for prey. All was silent. Jude began to feel better. He looked at the countryside spread out far beneath him. Streams sparkled like threads of silver, the sun winked off the tops of village houses, and, farther to the east, he could see...

What was that? A noise, from behind him, in the rocks! He jumped to his feet, and started to run. 'Fool!' he thought. 'Stopping like that in this countryside!' He ran desperately, feet skidding in the dust. He almost fell as he tripped over some small stones lying in the middle of the path.

Suddenly, there were men in front of him – men with dirty cloths tied over their mouths. Two of them grabbed him, holding him while the others hit him. He fell to the ground. Others tore off his clothes. 'Good cloth!' one of them muttered. 'He must be rich.'

Meanwhile, others had snatched his baggage, and had emptied it on the ground. They were sorting through his belongings. 'Not much in here, though!' one of them shouted, and kicked Jude. They picked up everything, and left.

Jude listened to the sound of their feet as they climbed through the loose gravel and rocks. Then all was silent once more. Above him, the eagle still circled, safe and far away. Jude tried to get up, but he couldn't. He felt weak and dizzy, and closed his eyes against the glare of the sun. 'Will anyone else come along? Will they be in time if they do?' he wondered. 'How long can I last up here in the heat? How long can I last without water?'

Already Jude was thirsty. It was still early in the afternoon. There were hours of the sun's heat to come. Jude thought about his wife, and how she had begged him not to travel that day alone. But he hadn't listened to her. He had laughed at her fears.

Suddenly, he heard a noise – the sound of sandals padding through the dust of the track. Who was it? He managed to lift his head so that he could see. It was a priest! 'Now I'll be safe!' he thought. He watched as the man drew nearer. 'He'll spot me soon, and rush to help me!' Jude thought.

The priest did spot him soon. 'Oh no!' he thought. 'A dead body! If I get too close to that, I won't be able to take part in the temple services tonight.' He quickly gathered up his rich robes, so that they wouldn't trail in the blood that had soaked into the dust on the ground. Carefully, he began to edge by the man lying across the track. As soon as he had passed him, he ran off as fast as he could.

So Jude was alone again. The sun beat down on him. His throat felt swollen and as dry as the dust around him. His ribs ached, and his face was sore.

Then, he heard the sound of singing! It sounded like one of the chants used in the Temple. The voice came nearer, and Jude could see that the singer was a Levite – one of the people who helped the priests in the Temple, and provided the music there. He was obviously practising for that day's services.

'Perhaps he will stop!' Jude thought. But the Levite took one look at him, and then ran away, even faster than the priest had done. Jude realized that the man was going to leave him. He begged, 'Please stop! Please help me!'
The Levite looked back at him, and then looked round nervously.

'I can't stop!' he said. 'The robbers will get me, too!' And he ran off, holding up his robes as he went. 'That's a good trick!' he thought. 'The robbers leave someone there and then just wait for someone like me to stop to help them. Then all they have to do is attack me too! Well, the trick didn't work this time!'

Jude couldn't believe that the two men had both left him. He thought about the men's faces as they had left him to die. How could anyone be that cruel? 'No one will stop to help me – even if anyone else comes this way!' he whispered. He closed his eyes. He was very tired. There was nothing he could do, and no one to help him.

But someone else was coming.
A donkey was picking its way
over the rough ground, its
ears flicking back now and
then as its rider talked to it.

Jude didn't hear the donkey coming. He didn't hear the man
rushing over when he saw Jude. But he felt the hand slide
gently under his neck, and the cool water at his lips. He heard
the voice whispering, 'Don't worry now, you're safe. I'm
Simeon. Here, have some water.' He drank thirstily, and then
lay there quietly while Simeon bathed the cuts and bruises on
his body. Then Simeon spoke again. 'Do you think you can
get up if I help you? I want to take you to a house I know.
They'll look after you there.'

Jude opened his eyes and looked at his rescuer. He saw his clothes and the decoration on them – and was amazed at what he saw. Simeon was a Samaritan! Now, Jude had grown up knowing that the Samaritans were enemies of the Jews. He had always been told that the Samaritans were no good, and would do all they could to harm the Jews – and here was a Samaritan helping him, a Jew.

Then he realized that Simeon probably didn't know he was a Jew. Perhaps he thought he was a Samaritan too. 'That must be what's happened!' he thought. 'If he finds out I'm a Jew, he'll soon be off.'

Simeon helped Jude on to his donkey and they set off slowly along the road. At last, they arrived at a small house by the side of a stream. The man living there obviously knew Simeon, for he rushed out to greet him. Together, they helped Jude inside, and on to a bed.

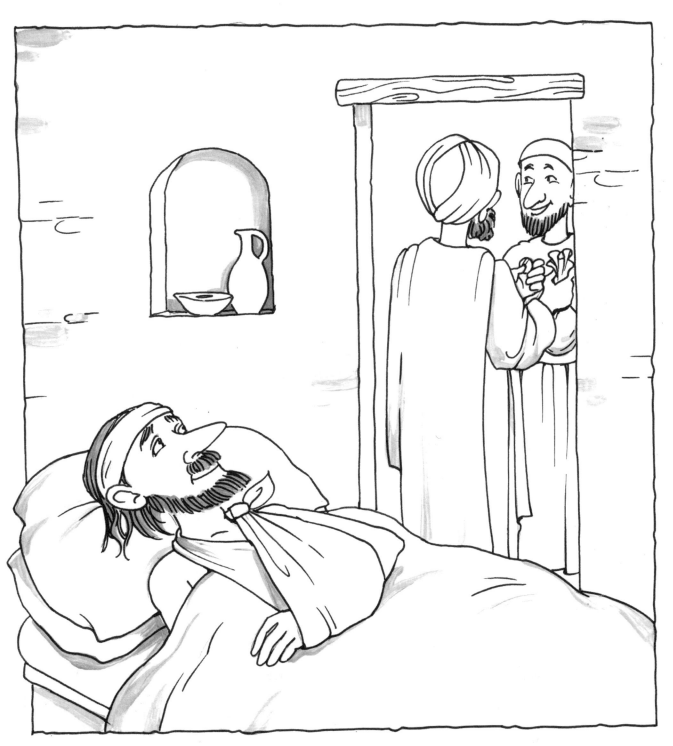

All that night, Simeon stayed with Jude, and looked after him, making him as comfortable as he could. Next morning, Jude woke up to hear Simeon talking to the owner of the house. He heard the clink of coins, and Simeon saying, 'This should be enough. Remember, buy all you need to help him recover, and look after him well. If you do spend any more, I'll pay you back next time I travel along this road.'

Jude couldn't believe how kind the man was. 'I have to tell him I'm a Jew!' he decided. 'It's not fair to trick him.' So he called Simeon over to him, and said, 'Thank you for all you've done for me. I have something to tell you that will make you angry. I'm a Jew.'

'Is that all?' Simeon said, laughing. 'I guessed you were probably a Jew when I stopped to help. It doesn't matter what you are. You needed help, and I was able to help you. That's all.'

Jude was amazed. Were all the things he had been told about Samaritans not true? This man had risked his own life to help him, just because he needed help. Simeon didn't care what country Jude came from, or what he believed in. All he cared about was helping him.

The owner of the house helped Jude to the door, so that he could wave goodbye to Simeon. Just before he disappeared round a bend in the road, Simeon turned in the saddle, and shouted, 'Jude, if you have to travel this way again, wait for me! Don't travel alone!'

Jude laughed. He was quite sure that he would never travel alone on that road again. But it would be good to meet Simeon again, and to get to know each other properly.

Activity Bank

Year 3

TERM 1

(W1) Revise long vowel phonemes: 'ee' – leads, green, meal, feel, beneath, heat, leave; 'ai' – safe, wave; 'ie' – hide, time, night, slide, side, buy; 'oa' – robes, soaked, throat, spoke, know, clothes, grown, road; 'oo' – Jude, smooth, cool, drew, soon.

(W8) Verbs ending with '-ing': chatting, struggling, scanning, stopping.

(W19) Examine words for dialogue: whispering, muttered, said, shouted, begged.

TERM 2

(W8) Explore 'y' + change: probably, angry.

(W10) Silent letters: climbed, know/knew, hours.

(W13) Explore suffixes: 'ly' – steeply, briskly, suddenly, properly, nervously, carefully, quickly, gently; 'ous' – dangerous; 'er' – rescuer, singer.

(W15) Contraction apostrophe: I'll, he'll, can't, I'm, won't, that's, didn't, don't, you're, what's.

TERM 3

(W11) Further contractions: couldn't (see Term 2).

(W14) Find homonyms: wave, set, leads, ground.

Year 4

TERM 1

(W6) Find homophones: their/there, sore/(saw), prey/(pray), more/(moor).

(W8) Irregular tense endings: try/tried, drank, was, saw, think/thought, can/could, leave/left.

TERM 2

(W11) Explore the way in which meanings change: rocky, wild, rich, sorted, track.

(W12) Define the following in set number of words: pray, rescuer, enemies, greet, trick.

(W13) Explore suffixes changing nouns to adjectives: dangerous, foolish, rocky, comfortable.

TERM 3

(W6) Same letter strings, different pronunciation: 'ou'/'ough' – could, shouted, ground, through, thought, rough; 'ea' – spread, beneath.

(W9) Explore suffixes: comfortable.

(W10) Look at possessive/contraction: its/it's.

(W11) Compound words: farmland, something, someone, hillside, countryside.

Year 3

TERM 1

(S3b) Classify verbs: see Word level Term 1 (W19).

(S4) Irregular tense changes: take/took, leave/left, think/thought, fall/fell, hear/heard.

(S6) Look at ! and ?: paragraph beginning, 'Suddenly, he heard a noise…'.

TERM 2

(S2c) Adjective substitution: for good, rich.

(S4) Look at singular and plural forms: regular; irregular – man/men, enemy/enemies.

TERM 3

(S5) Complex conjunctions: however, so, while.

(S6) Time sequences: then, meanwhile, at last.

Year 4

TERM 1

(S2) Revise verb tenses.

(S3) Look at powerful verbs: snaked, snatched, grabbed, shouted, begged, tore.

(S4a) Adverbs with 'ly': steeply, carefully, gently, nervously, briskly, desperately, harshly.

TERM 2

(S1) Revise adjectives; figurative and expressive language: snaked, winked, sandals padding; similes: like threads of silver, dry as the dust.

(S2b) Look at possessive apostrophe, singular and plural: sun's heat, man's hand/men's faces.

(S2c) Explore possessive/contraction apostrophes: see above and Year 3, Word level, Term 2 (W15) – it's/its.

TERM 3

(S2) Look at the use of colons, semi-colons, commas, dashes and speech marks: two

▶

paragraphs beginning, 'What was that?' (pages 9–10)

(S3a) Examine changing word order: sentence beginning, 'High above him…'

Text level

Year 3

TERM 1

(T4, 5, 14) Explore the difference between prose and a playscript, writing own playscripts.

Class: Talk about differences between prose and playscript. What is needed to turn prose into playscript? Which do they think would be the better way of communicating this story and why? Introduce Worksheet A.
Group: Pupils work through Worksheet A in pairs.
Plenary: Some pairs read out their scripts: do they work as scripts?

TERM 2

(T3, 8) Look at characters: evaluate behaviour and write portraits of them.

Class: Together, discuss the characters and motivation of Jude, Simeon, the priest and the Levite, using textual evidence. Brainstorm words to describe each, collecting them around enlarged pictures. Pupils can copy words on to Worksheet C as you write. Introduce group task.
Group: Pupils, as a character from the story, write a letter to a friend about another character—for example, Jude writing about the good Samaritan. The letter must show the person's character as revealed in the story, and explain what the character did as well as what he is like.
Plenary: Read some letters and evaluate them: are the people accurately described?

TERM 3

(T3, 12) Examine how we distinguish between first- and third-person accounts; changing third- into first-person account.

Class: Discuss the differences between first- and third-person accounts. Discuss which form can have more impact. Ask pupils how an incident from the story (such as the good Samaritan's arrival) would be written if in the first person. Point out that a person might give a very different account if speaking for himself.
Group: Pupils adopt the persona of a chosen character and retell the story (or part of it).

Plenary: Pupils read out their accounts without saying who they are. Can the others identify them?

Year 4

TERM 1

(T1, 2, 11) Look at the way characters are built up from small details, evoking sympathy/dislike. Write character sketches.

Class: Using Worksheet C, brainstorm words to describe Jude and the Levite, and write them around the pictures. Ask the pupils whether they feel sympathy or dislike for each one and why. Write this evidence around the pictures. Circle the words which evoke sympathy and underline the ones evoking dislike.
Group: Pupils do the same for one other character. They write a character sketch based on this work, considering whether they are trying to evoke sympathy, dislike or both.
Plenary: Pupils read out their sketches. Others evaluate their accuracy and the use of details to evoke a response.

TERM 2

(T2, 4, 5, 10, 13) Look at settings and their influence; adjectives, expressive and descriptive language and its effects; figurative language including similes.

Class: Annotate one of the passages on Worksheet D with the pupils, marking use of any of the devices you wish to consider. Talk about how the setting is built up and how it influences the characters.
Group: Annotate the rest of the passages. On the back, pupils write their own description of the setting.
Plenary: Identify devices found. Read some of their descriptions.

TERM 3

(T3) Explore the use of paragraphs.

Class: Talk about the need for and the rules of paragraphing. Look at a section of the story and decide why each new paragraph starts where it does, identifying topics and noting change of speaker. (NB: The text uses just one correct way of paragraphing the material.)
Group: On Worksheet E, pupils mark where they believe paragraphs should start, indicating the reason, and summing up the meaning/topic of each paragraph.
Plenary: Compare arrangement of paragraphing, and comment on correctness.

Literacy Worksheet A

Here is a passage from the story:

> Jude thought about his wife, and how she had begged him not to travel that day alone. But he hadn't listened to her. He had laughed at her fears.

This is how it could be written as a playscript:

> **Ruth:** You know how dangerous that road is.
> Please don't go, Jude!
> **Jude:** You're being silly.
> **Ruth:** (crying) I'm not! Please stay at home.
> **Jude:** (laughing) I'd look silly then! I'm off. Goodbye!

Activity 1
Mark the differences between the two.

Activity 2
Now choose another scene and write it out as a playscript in the box below. You could use the scene between the house owner and the good Samaritan, or you could imagine what the good Samaritan and Jude talked about when they met the next time.

Literacy Worksheet B

Here are some speeches from the story:

'Please stop!' Jude begged.

'I can't stop!' the Levite said. 'The robbers will get me too!'

'I have something to tell you,' Jude said.

'Is that all?' Simon said, laughing.

Activity 1
Using coloured pencils, mark the following:
★ Underline the full stops in red.
★ Underline the commas in blue.
★ Circle exclamation and question marks in black.
★ Circle the capital letters in brown.

Notice when all these are used.
Notice when a new paragraph begins — every time there is a new speaker.

Activity 2
Use what you have found out to put in the punctuation and capital letters in these speeches between Jude and his wife Ruth.

are you going alone said Ruth i will be all right he said please don't go Ruth said you're being silly Jude said

Can you think of any other words for 'said' that would make this passage more interesting to read? For instance, you could use 'asked' for the first 'said'.
You could also add adverbs to show how the people were speaking (for example, 'unhappily').

Teacher's note
The first set of speeches could be used for later work on direct and indirect speech.

Literacy Worksheet C

Activity 1
In a colour, write around their pictures words to describe the characters.

Activity 2
In another colour, write around the pictures the words and events which tell you about each character.

Jude

Good
Samaritan

Priest

Levite

Activity 3
Decide whether these words/events make you feel sympathy or dislike for each character. Circle the words/events which make you feel sympathy. Underline the words/events which make you feel dislike.

Literacy Worksheet D

Activity 1

Choose one passage from those below.
Annotate it, commenting on two of the following:
★ similes   ★ description of setting
★ figurative language ★ adjectives
★ adverbs   ★ details

(A) It was a wild and dangerous track. It snaked along the rocky hillsides, climbing so steeply that travellers had no breath left for chatting.

(B) High above him an eagle circled, scanning the rocks below for prey. All was silent. Jude began to feel better. He looked at the countryside spread out far beneath him. Streams sparkled like threads of silver, the sun winked off the tops of village houses, and, farther to the east, he could see...

(C) He ran desperately, feet skidding in the dust. He almost fell as he tripped over some small stones lying in the middle of the path.

(D) So Jude was alone again. The sun beat down on him. His throat felt swollen and as dry as the dust around him.

(E) But someone else was coming. A donkey was picking its way over the rough ground, its ears flicking back now and then as its rider talked to it. Jude didn't hear the donkey coming. He didn't hear the man rushing over when he saw Jude. But he felt the hand slide gently under his neck, and the cool water at his lips.

Activity 2

Use some of these devices to write your own description of the setting of the story. You can use the back of this sheet of paper.

Literacy Worksheet E

Activity

Read the text below. Then complete the two tasks.

★ With a coloured pencil, mark where you think new paragraphs could start. The first one is done for you (in black).

★ Write at the side of four of the marks the reason for starting a new paragraph there.

So Jude was alone again. The sun beat down on him. His throat felt swollen and as dry as the dust around him. His ribs ached, and his face was sore. // Then, he heard the sound of singing! Jude could see that the singer was a Levite. He was obviously practising for that day's services. 'Perhaps he will stop!' Jude thought. But the Levite took one look at him, and then ran away, even faster than the priest had done. Jude realized that the man was going to leave him. He begged, 'Please stop! Please help me!' The Levite looked back at him, and then looked round nervously. 'I can't stop!' he said. 'The robbers will get me, too!' And he ran off, holding up his robes as he went. 'That's a good trick!' he thought. 'The robbers leave someone there and then just wait for someone like me to stop to help them. Then all they have to do is attack me too! Well, the trick didn't work this time!' Jude couldn't believe that the two men had both left him. 'No one will stop to help me—even if anyone else comes this way!' he whispered. He closed his eyes.

RE Teacher's Page

The story 'Who cares?' is based on the parable of the good Samaritan (Luke 10:25–37).

Story framework

To use this story in RE, introduce it in the following format: 'Once, Jesus was talking about the verse which says people should love and look after their neighbour in the same way as they look after themselves. Someone asked Jesus, "But who is my neighbour?" So Jesus told this story.'

Read the story.

'Jesus told this story to show that anyone who needs help is our neighbour – not just the people who live nearby or the person we like and agree with.'

Background material

The people of Samaria and the Jews had been enemies for many years. The Jews believed that the Samaritans were impure in both race and religion, and did not allow them to worship at the Temple in Jerusalem. So the Samaritans built their own Temple. Each race tried to avoid the other, and some Jews would even risk the dangers of the road the traveller used to avoid passing through Samaria. Jesus travelled freely through both countries, and stopped to help a woman in Samaria.

The priests performed the ritual duties in the Temple – the services of worship and prayer, and the sacrifices. They also taught and interpreted the Mosaic Law. The Levites assisted the priests, and were responsible for the music in the Temple. Under Mosiac Law, both groups were made unclean by contact with a dead body, and so would have been able to resume their duties only after long rituals. The priest and the Levite were right to fear for their own safety: the Samaritan helped the traveller at risk to his own life.

The road led along a very steep valley side, and was well known as a haunt for robbers.

The 'inn' would probably have been a private house: hospitality was very important to the Jews.

Conversation starters

★ Using the background information as necessary, discuss why the priest and the Levite did not stop to help.
★ Was it easy for the Samaritan to stop and help? What did it cost him – apart from money? What sort of help did he give – emergency and/or long-term help?

★ What would the Jews in the audience have been expecting to happen? How would any Samaritans in the audience have felt at the end of the story?
★ Ask for some definitions of the word 'neighbour' in a set number of words – under ten, for example.

Religious Education

RE activities

The pupils will need to know about the enmity between the Jews and the Samaritans.

BASIC

(Use an enlarged figure of the good Samaritan, mounted on a sheet of paper, from Literacy Worksheet C.) On one label, write what the Jews thought the Samaritan was like and how they thought he would act, and attach this to the outside of the figure. On a second label, write what he was really like and how he really acted, and attach this on the inside of the figure. This is a story Jesus told, but people often label others wrongly when they don't know them. Write a short story in which someone whom you thought was an enemy turns out to be a friend.

STANDARD

As above, but go on to think about why people label others wrongly, and write these reasons round the picture. Inside the picture, write your suggestions about how people can try to put the right labels on others.

EXTENSION

Re-read the story within its framework, imagining that you are either a Samaritan or a Jew listening to Jesus. Write a letter to your relations in another town, telling them about Jesus and his teaching, and telling them how this story has changed your thinking about neighbours and about Jews and Samaritans.

Reflection/Learning from religion

The Jews would not have expected a Samaritan to help a Jew. They did not look at the real people, but just labelled them as 'Samaritans – our enemies'. It is easy to judge someone before we know anything about them. Do you label people before you really know them? How can you get to know what people are really like?

Activity 1

Make a neighbours wheel using instructions 1, 2 and 3 overleaf. The people listening to Jesus thought that their neighbours were only:

★ the people living near to them. (Write 'people living near' in one of the segments.)
★ the people in their country. (Write 'people in this country' in another segment.)
★ the people who shared their beliefs. (Write 'people with the same beliefs' in another segment.)

Activity 2

Jesus said that their neighbour was:

★ anyone in any country, anywhere, who needed help. (Write 'people in another country' in another segment.)
★ anyone with different beliefs, who needed help. (Write 'people who don't have the same belief' in a segment.)
★ anyone who needed help, even their enemy. (Write 'enemies who need help' in another segment.)
★ anyone who needed help. (Write 'anyone who needs help' in the last segment.)

Activity 3

★ In the outer circle, write 'neighbours' several times around the circle. Colour each sector a different, bright colour.
★ Follow the instructions on 'The neighbours wheel' activity sheet.

Think about it

Christians believe that Jesus wants them to look after anyone who needs help, whoever they are. All of the groups on the wheel are really in one group – they are all neighbours. When the wheel is spun, the different colours become just one colour. Christians believe that this is how Jesus wants them to think about other people – not in groups of people they might or might not like, but just as people who may need their help.

The neighbours wheel

Instructions

1. Cut out a circle 10cm in diameter and glue it on to card.
2. Teacher: pierce holes as marked.

3. Thread a length of string about 70cm long through the holes and knot to make a loop. (Do not use nylon thread or similar, as this may cut hands.)
4. Hold the thread as shown.
5. 'Wind up' the disc (this can be done by rolling the disc along the table, or along the pupil's leg or chest). Gently space hands apart to put tension on string, but release tension just before string untwists.
6. Keep string slack until it winds in opposite direction. Apply tension again, so that disc spins in opposite direction. Continue until movement has died away.
7. Watch coloured circle as it spins. Think about how the different groups of people, each on their own colour, have disappeared into one colour. In this parable, Jesus was saying that we should not just look at the differences between us, but that we should help others when they need help.

Teacher's note

If appropriate, the pupils can be directed to use the seven colours of the rainbow for the wheel, for work on colour.